Lil Legends

First learning book of

wild animals

lion

elephant

tiger

fox

deer

leopard

bear

zebra

giraffe

hippopotamus

kangaroo

hyena

koala

rhinoceros

monkey

porcupine

wolf

panda

snake

gorilla

lion

elephant

tiger

fox

deer

leopard

bear

zebra

giraffe

hippo-
potamus

kangaroo

hyena

koala

rhinoceros

monkey

porcupine

wolf

panda

snake

gorilla

Lil Legends

VOTED PRODUCT OF THE YEAR
Consumer Survey of Product Innovation
2025

Designed for little hands and curious minds, Lil Legends Picture Board books are colourful treasures that foster observation and vocabulary skills in young learners. These beautifully crafted and sturdy books are invitations to explore, learn and grow. Open the pages and let the learning adventure begin!

* Winner Writing Books for Children Category.
Survey of 1800 people by NielsenIQ across categories.

Printed at Azure Press Pvt. Ltd., Bahadurgarh-124507, Haryana

Lil Legends
An imprint of
OSWAAL BOOKS

Head Office, Oswaal House
1/11, Sahitya Kunj, M.G. Road,
Agra (U.P.) India-282002

0562-2857671
contact@oswaalbooks.com
www.lillegendsbooks.com

ISBN
9789359586731

India	INR ₹	99.00
Abroad	USD $	5.00
	CAD $	6.00

Lil Legends wild animals